# Insidious by Design

## Lyrics on Race

sabrina brancato

MELTING POèT

White supremacy is […] insidious by design. The racism
required to uphold white supremacy is woven into every area
of our lives.
(Ijeoma Oluo)

The politics of whiteness transcends the colour of anyone's
skin. It is an occupying force in the mind. It is a political
ideology that is concerned with maintaining power through
domination and exclusion. Anyone can buy into it, just like
anyone can choose to challenge it.
(Reni Eddo-Lodge)

We must continue to ask *how* our racism manifests, not *if*.
(Robin DiAngelo)

For Kainene Daphnée and Ayodele Junior,
my beloved children

May your future be bright
and your confidence never stumble

*Where Whiteness Fears to Tread: Lyrics on Race*, published in 2020, was my first reflection on the oppressive power of Whiteness in a poetic form. This book is a follow-up. You can read one without having read the other, though they do speak to and complement each other. One can and must always go a step further into the exploration of the pervasiveness of the "invisible race".

Credit goes to the powerful voices that have inspired me and that inhabit my mind and soul, guiding me through and accompanying my falling out of Whiteness. This is where I really come from: James Baldwin more than any other, Steve Biko, Maryse Condé, Angela Davis, Birago Diop, Bernardine Evaristo, Frantz Fanon, Zora Neale Hurston, Lynton Kwesi Johnson, Jamaica Kincaid, Audre Lorde, Toni Morrison, Grace Nichols, Claudia Rankine, Benjamin Zephaniah, and many other freedom fighters.

I also come from two parents who were largely unaware of racism in its most subtle forms, but who taught me compassion and offered me a lot of books, enough to open the door for antiracism to reach me.

1.

Am I being fragile
I ask myself
Am I being
Fragile
When I walk away
From long days
Of being placed
Under fire
Am I being
Fragile

You call me
Becky
Karen
Coloniser
Supremacist
You say
My writing is
Garbage
Minstrel show
Pure crap
You accuse me
Of using
My children
MY CHILDREN
As a tool
Of marketing
You ask me

Whom I am crediting
Whom I am compensating
You spit on me
From afar
And you would
Spit on me
Literally
If you were here
If I were there
And sure
You have
Your reasons
And I thought
In all these years
I had built
Some tolerance
For discomfort
In order to
Really
Listen
And yet

Oh no
Am I being fragile
When I walk away
Because
No matter how hard
I try
To engage in
A conversation

To acknowledge
Your reasons
Your point of view
To explain
My reasons
My point of view
Which is only mine
Because in spite of
What you think
I am not pretending
To speak for you
Not even for my children
No
Not even for them
I am not pretending
To occupy a space
Which I know is
And must be
Yours
I am not trying
To profit
From this
Because
This is not
A business
In my view
But a duty
A moral obligation
You keep
Spitting on me

Again
And again
And again

Am I being fragile
Am I being defensive
Am I derailing
Am I tone policing
When I ask you
To please stop calling me
Epithets
And phrase your criticism
Which I take seriously
Without insulting
Because I still
Want to listen to
What you
Have to say

Bloody supremacist
Is picking on language
The other says
Bloody supremacist
Is using her privilege
Bloody supremacist
Is being fragile

Am I being fragile
When I walk away
Because you think

I should not
Write
About
Race
Being a
Becky
Karen
Coloniser
Supremacist
But I still want to
Write
About
Race
Am I being
Fragile

Yes
Maybe
I am
Being
Fragile
And
This
Is
Still
Part
Of the process
Of learning

I am walking away

But I am not
Giving up
Precisely because
This is
Not at all
About
Myself

Whites should not be afraid of being called out on their participation in the dynamics of oppression. It is okay to be called into question. A white person writing about race will inevitably make mistakes, as our perspective is necessarily limited. Nevertheless, this is not a reason to withdraw from the struggle. On the contrary, it is an occasion for further reflection. If I open this collection precisely with this poem, it is not to place the focus on my own emotions, but to highlight the contradictions inherent to my own position. This unpleasant exchange, experienced on social media shortly after the publication of *Where Whiteness Fears to Tread*, triggered ambivalent emotions and actually sparked the fuel for this new book, what is more than sufficient proof of my own "flammability", a term proposed by Sun Yung Shin as an alternative to Robin DiAngelo's "white fragility".

2.

Black
Solitude
Is
Oceanic

I came across these words
Years ago
And they struck me
As so painfully true

Black
Solitude
Is
Oceanic

How can
Such a short
Statement
Contain
Centuries
Of history
From the chains
Of the Atlantic
To the graves
Of the Mediterranean

How can it
Convey

So much
In so little

The frustration
The disillusionment
The distress
The strength
The resilience
The loud struggles
And the silent ones

Black
Solitude
Is
Oceanic

So insightful
It taught me more
Than hundred books

So powerful
It stayed with me
And settled deep

Black
Solitude
Is
Oceanic

It resonates

Every time
Race remains
Unexamined
Every time
Abuse is left
Unpunished
Every time
Whiteness
Reaffirms
Its power
Which is to say
It resonates
All the time
Like my own
Heartbeat

It resonates
Now
That racism
Does no longer
Make
Headlines
Now
That the names
Of the murdered
Are no longer
Spelt aloud
Now
That improvised
Allies

Have vanished
And BLM t-shirts
Have been packed away
In the drawers
Of our hypocrisy

Black
Solitude
Is
Oceanic

Oceanic

And this ocean
Is
So wide
So deep




This poem was inspired by an artwork I saw years ago in the
context of the exhibition "Entre terra e mar. Between Land
and Sea. Transatlantic Art" at the Weltkulturen Museum in
Frankfurt am Main. The exhibition, curated by Jane de
Hohenstein and Mona B. Suhrbier, featured the work of
Ayrson Heráclito, Doté Amilton Costa, Gilmar Tavares and
other artists. I am very grateful to the curators for granting
me the right to include the photograph of the art piece in
this book. The phrase is from the "dividing poem" by
Wlamyra Albuquerque.

BLACK SOLITUDE IS OCEANIC

3.

A five-year old
Shouting
Racial slurs
At an older girl
Coming to his rescue
In a moment of distress
Says it all
About the monstrosity
Of the system
We've set up

Even amidst
Highest
Palpable
Danger
The biggest
Threat
Whiteness
Perceives
Is
Black
Skin

4.

The teacher
Had to intervene
Several times
In order to stop
My daughter's "best" friend
From calling her names

The little girl insisted
That *negrita*
Is not
Racist

This went on
Over several days
During which
She double-checked
With her parents
And came back
Reinforced
In her conviction
And outraged
At being called out

The whole thing
Only stopped
When the teacher
Finally
Applied sanctions

And made clear
To all the class
That this
Is not
Acceptable

It took
Too long
And nothing
Can compensate
The bruises left
On my daughter's
Emotions

When it comes to racism
I wish we would stop
Placing the focus
On what whiteness considers
Right or wrong

Why should we care
About the offender's opinions
More than we do
About the harm caused

School is
No private space
And if it boasts
As it does
To combat racism

It should act
Quick
And forthright
In stopping
Any expression
Of bigotry
And teach children
That respect
Must have priority
Over personal opinions

5.

Oh no
He didn't mean it
Said the mother
No, of course he didn't
They are such good friends
Said the other
Sure he didn't mean it
Said the teacher
Let's forget this
Said all
Parroting each other
        forget
                forget
                        forget
*Daos un besito*
*Y amigos como antes*
Friends again

What did you say
Wait
What did you say

The little boy
Has been spitting
A racial epithet
On his classmate
Over several days
And they're saying she

Should get over it
They're saying he
Did not mean it

Why should she
Care
What he meant
Why are they
Addressing her
And asking her
To excuse
And forget
Instead of
Addressing him
And asking him
To make amends
And apologise

I tell you why
Because the racism
This little boy is
Expressing
Is the racism we
Legitimise
Every time
We give space
To the intentions
Of the offender
Instead of sanctioning
The act itself

For what it is
And mind you
All this understanding
On our part
All this empathy
With the offender
Is nothing more
Than the proof
Of how much racism
We carry
In ourselves

6.

But in the end
The problem
Is not
The racial slur
Hurled openly
In the school yard
Or at the train station
(Because you know your worth
And your confidence does not stumble)

The problem
Is not even
The one
Disguised
As a compliment
And meant to
Have you
Fit in the box
Reserved
For people
Your colour
(Because you know better
And your confidence does not stumble)

The real problem
Is the one
That you don't hear
The one

Never pronounced aloud
The one
Concealed
In the meanders
Of the subconscious
Of the disproportionate number
Of well-meaning whites
Holding the reins
Of your life

Teachers
Doctors
Trainers
Carers
Examiners
Social workers
Therapists
Family friends
Sometimes even
Parents

That is the problem
Because you trust them
And most of them
Genuinely believe
They are acting
In your best interest

7.

Dear
White
People
Why don't we
Stop
Taking it
So
Personally
When we are
Called out on
Racism

Why
Is it
So difficult
To see
That this is not
About
Ourselves

It is a cage
We are all
Trapped in

All this talking
About
Thinking
Out of the box

And then
We are
Not even able
To imagine
A world
Out of the cage

So afraid
Are we
Of letting go
That we punch in the face
The one who shows us
The way out

Dear
White
People
Next time
It happens
Please
Just pause
And take
Your time
To think about it
Because
There is
Always
Another way
Of looking
At things

8.

You all seem to think
We are
Making
Too much
Far too much
Out of it

But imagine
Just imagine
What it must be like

All that prejudice
Thrown at you
All that negativity
Thrown at you
All that hatred
Thrown at you
All that stupidity
Thrown at you

Imagine
Just imagine
What it must feel like

Being pinched
Being punched
Being stung
Being smacked

Being debased
Being degraded
Being discredited
Being defamed

Being brutalised
Being stigmatised
Being exploited
Being abused

Being undervalued
Being misconceived
Being disregarded
Being erased

Imagine
Just imagine

Because
That is precisely
What racism
Feels like

9.

Say his name
Eleazar Blandón
Is no less a victim
Of racism
Than George Floyd
Yet
Where is
The outcry
Why
Aren't we
Taking
To the streets
No justice
No peace
Black Lives Matter
Will not be
Our badge
Until
We acknowledge
Homegrown racism
Right under our noses
The sweetness
Of the watermelon
At our kitchen table
Would speak volumes
If we would only
Listen
And recognise

The bitterness
Of the many lives
Men
Women
Youngsters
Forced to work
In the fields
Under extreme heat
Not given water
Not given rest
Maltreated
Denigrated
Eleazar
Left to die
Like his father
Shortly before him
Where is
The outcry
For modern slavery
Made in the EU
Say his name
Eleazar Benjamín Blandón Herrera
Spell it loud
Let it resonate
At your kitchen table
In the fields
At the marketplace
For all
Who have come
Looking

For a better life
For all
Who have been
Stolen
To their families
For all
Whose blood
Is running
In the juicy
Watermelon
At our kitchen table

HIGH LINE ZOO

10.

In the shop window
My daughter spotted
A small figurine
Of a Black bride
Standing alone
Among tons of
White
Bride-and-groom
Cake toppers
She said Mama please
And I went inside
To purchase it
This goes with discount
As she lost her groom
Said the guy at the counter
Very pretty isn't she
Yes I said
Very pretty indeed
Just like you
Said the guy
Handing the figurine
To my little girl
And I paid
Happy to see my child
Holding her Black bride Black pride
And going home
To show everybody
Her beautiful self

In wedding dress
Not caring at all
About the missing groom
Then displayed
The lonely bride
On a shelf
Has been there since
And none of us
Has ever worried
About her loneliness
Until today
Today
I've come across
The US statistics
Of groups
Unwillingly unmarried
Namely
Asian men and
Black women
As a consequence of
Their counterparts
Choosing
White partners
And the words resonate
In my head
This goes with a discount
As she lost her groom
Lost her groom
Lost her groom
And suddenly

A pretty figurine
On a shelf
Carries a meaning
Beyond itself
Suddenly
Her loneliness
Is real
Painful
That's how insidious
Race can be
When
Not even cake toppers
Are spared

11.

As a matter of fact
I generally
Do not
Appreciate
Whites
Sporting
Typically Black
Hairstyles
One of many
Forms
Of appropriation
And just
One more
Unrecognised
Form
Of racism

Yet today
This one policeman
With dark hair
And perfectly styled
Cornrows
Winking at my children
And greeting them
With a bright smile
Makes me hopeful
That things
Might

Change
For the better

At this stage in history
And in his position
I read his hairstyle
As a message
Of reassurance
A sign
That he cares

Maybe I am being naïve
In my hope
That a police officer
Might stand
With BLM

Maybe my white self
Is drawing
Too rosy a picture
But at this stage in history
And in our position
I need to read
His cornrows
As a statement

Because at this stage in history
Whatever your position
Neutrality
Is not

Acceptable

Because at this stage in history
Whatever your position
You need
To make clear
Where
You
Stand

Especially
If you are
White

12.

A friend sends me
A short article
Announcing the decision
Of a French publisher
To modify the title
Of a popular book
By Agatha Christie
Removing
The infamous word
From the title
As well as from
The text

My friend asks me
What I think of it

I say in principle
It is something to be done
However late
(British editions
Have done so
Four decades ago!)
But I hesitate
To celebrate
Such actions
Because replacing words
Does not erase
The racism

Underlying
The narrative
If anything
It only makes it
Less visible
And therefore
Probably
Even more
Insidious

I hesitate
To celebrate
Such actions
Unless they come
With a critical
Introduction
Because
If you do not
Speak of
Race
You do nothing more
Than
Reinforcing it

Then
It downs on me
I have overlooked
A crucial detail
The article says
The title will be

Changed
In order
Not to
Hurt
Some
People
But
This sounds
To me
As a confirmation
Of a racist stance
Because hey
Antiracism
Means (should mean)
We acknowledge
To live in a world
Permeated by
Racism
And we
Want it to be
Different
So we take action
For the benefit
Of all

Again
This is not
About
Some
People

Feeling hurt
This is about
Dismantling
The structure
We are
All
Trapped in

And yes
Were I not
Imbued with
Whiteness
I would not
Have overlooked
This detail
In the first place

13.

In this strange new world
In which we are to wear masks
In public spaces
And keep a distance
From each other
Unless we live
Under the same roof
We are finally spared
From having to tell
Any other stranger
Or barely familiar person
DON'T touch MY hair

It has taken a pandemic
To reach this stage
To grant our body
The right
To privacy

14.

First day of school
For my 3<sup>rd</sup> graders
The kids are so excited
When I go fetch them
First thing they say
There is a new girl
In their class
And she is
Black

Pizza is waiting for us
On the kitchen table
And I feel like opening
A bottle of champagne

Every single new Black child
In this far too white school
Is a reason
For celebration

The day they'll have
A Black teacher
(make it happen!)
I'll get myself drunk

15.

Black Beethoven
Is not about
Beethoven being
Black
It is about
Our children knowing
That the Black presence
Is not new
To this continent
It is about
Our children knowing
That people their ancestry
Made Europe
Made Western culture
As much as others did
Black Beethoven
Is about
Who gets
Into the canon
And who does not
It is about
Samuel Coleridge-Taylor
Not being taught and talked about
As much as his white peers
It is about
Julius Eastman
Dying homeless
It is about

White-washing
At all levels of culture
It is about
Alexandre Dumas
Being impersonated
By Depardieu
It is about
Black inventors
Never being named
It is about
Whiteness
Dictating the rules
It is about
Whiteness
Making Black excellence
Invisible
It is about
Looking
Into what has been lost
It is about
Black people
Reclaiming their place of honour
In a history
That has passed
For white
Only

16.

These stories
I'm watching
With my children
In order to improve
Their English
Are supposed to be
Empowering
The British Council
Has made the big step
Of bringing diversity
Into our imaginary
Of what being British
Looks like
And so their website
Of English for kids
Features faces
Of many colours
And yet
When you see
Black faces
Portrayed as kings and queens
Black characters
In untroubled relationships
With white ones
Black children
As Shakespeare's classmates
You get it all wrong
You are made to believe

You, child
Raised in colour-blindness
That racism is
An invention
Of a few crazy guys
That British history
Was all so peaceful
That interracial relationships
Were no trouble at all
That Blacks
Could
Be
In power
If only they wanted
You see
Don't you see
How tricky
Your anti-racism can be
When it erases
The history
And reality
Of racism
You see
Don't you see
That when you bring race
Into the picture
Without bringing racism
Into it
You are doing no more
Than

Reinforcing
Your power
Because
If you don't teach
Our children
How things
Really
Were
They'll have no tools
To understand
And transform
What they live
Today

17.

There are many ways
Black skin is
More vulnerable
Than white one

Many ways
A Black mother is
More vulnerable
Than a white one

Many ways
A Black child is
More vulnerable
Than a white one

Thinking of you
Belly Mujinga
And the loneliness
Of your little girl
Left motherless
By a system
That has made
Both of you
More vulnerable
Than others

Your death
Dear Belly

Speaks volumes

Your life
Dear Belly
Until your last breath
Is the book
Of inequality
The book that tells us
We still have
So much to learn
So much to do
For justice
To be real

Belly Mujinga
Died alone

Her daughter
Could not say
Goodbye

Her husband
Could not say
Goodbye

Her friend
Could not say
Goodbye

And it was too late

Too late

She was not supposed
To be at work
In her conditions

What are you doing here
Yelled the man
And without knowing
The offender
Was right

You were not supposed
To be there
Vulnerable
Unprotected
Exposed

Had he not
Spat on you
You would still
Have died

The guilt
Stays
With the ones
Who did not
Protect you
The ones
Who refused

To let you go

To your home
To your child
To your life

In safety

18.

And there is always
A double conversation
Going on

The one
Coming out
Of my mouth
Which strives
To be civil
Without really
Bringing us
Forward

And the one
In my head
Naked truth
Which would not
Bring us forward
Either

And both
Have a bitter
Such a bitter
Taste

19.

White-child-me
Is 9 years old
When the family
Ventures North
For summer holidays

Oh, you talk funny
But of course you
Down there
You're all Africans
*Tutti africani*
*Laggiù siete tutti*
*Africani*

(North meaning
200 kilometres
upward from Naples
yet still south
of Rome)

Oh, you talk funny
But of course you
Down there
*Tutti africani*
*Laggiù siete tutti*
*Africani*

On the day

She is introduced
To a group of
Boys and girls
White-child-me is shy
But no more than usual

Oh, you talk funny
But of course you
*Tutti africani*
*Laggiù siete tutti*
*Africani*

It is the laughter
Which hurts the most
Not the words
The laughter
Will make her think twice
Before opening her mouth again
But the words
Are instructive

Oh, you talk funny
But of course you
*Tutti africani*
*Laggiù siete tutti*
*Africani*

She learns
That she
Has an accent

And she learns
That her accent
Is not
The right one
And she learns
That her hometown
Is not widely appreciated
As she thought it should be
And she learns
That Africa
Is not widely appreciated
As she was taught it should be

Oh, you talk funny
*Tutti africani*
*Laggiù siete tutti*
*Africani*

And she wonders why
Those kids say African
With such scorn
It their voice
And such cruelty
In their laughter

*Tutti africani*
*Laggiù siete tutti*
*Africani*

African is papa's younger friend

She secretly has a crush on
(dear diary he is so beautiful
let me grow up soon)
African are the children
Granma brings in
At every single meal
(do not dare leave a crumble
in your dish
show respect for the ones
not lucky as you)
African is the big hair
Of that lady called
Free Angela
On uncle C's door
(uncle C is doing his best
but his hair will never grow
as big as hers)
African is the round black face
On the chocolate candies
Auntie M carries in her bag
(you get one if you behave
when guests come visit
two if you keep still and quiet
all through Sunday mass)
African is her first
And foremost TV hero
(the family sit together
in silence and awe
when Kunta Kinte is on screen)
African is the map

Of that huge place
Mum says is
The cradle of humanity
(which sounds difficult
but must mean
goodness
comes from there)

*Laggiù siete tutti*
*Africani*

Words are
Food for thought
And that day
Out of the blue
White-child-me
Learns
She
Is African
Too

Words are
Food for thought
And one day
White-child-me
Will learn to wear
As a badge of honour
Her Whiteness
Of a different colour

Words are
Food for thought
And from that day
White-child-me
Will take pride
In challenging racism
Large and wide

(That was
Growing up
In the seventies
In a divided country
With a colour line
Of its own)

20.

I was that little girl
Who wanted to be
A ballerina
That little girl
Who was so happy
When her mother
Enrolled her
In a ballet school
That little girl
Who was so excited
When after a year of training
She made her first appearance
On a theatre stage
Dancing a mazurka
That little girl
Whose dreams were crushed
When after another year of training
She was shoved
Onto the same stage
Wearing a tight overall
Dark brown
And a straw skirt
Her face hands and feet
Smeared with
A dark brown sticky cream
Her hair concealed
By a wig
Of short black kinky hair

And to top it all
A fruit basket
On her head
I was that little girl
Who was so revolted
By her grotesque disguise
She stumbled all over the place
Having the fruit roll over
And left the stage in tears
I was that little girl
Who had never heard of racism
And yet already knew
What it looked and felt like
And that was the end
Of my ballet career

21.

White-child-me is
Holding her first baby doll
In her arms
Baby is black
And so sweet and beautiful
White-child-me
Carries baby everywhere
Kisses baby all over
Runs her fingers softly
Through baby's curly hair
Dresses and undresses baby
Sings baby lullabies
Loves baby as only
A 5-year-old mother can love
White-child-me is happy
And so proud
Of her baby

Many years later
Growing critical
Of the exotic edge
In race relations
I came to be ashamed
Of that first motherly love
But today
Looking back
I wonder
If that present

From my mum
Wasn't actually
Her most precious
Gift to her daughter
A lesson of love
And counterculture

She chose
That one baby doll
For me
No other
And it was
My only one
Baby doll
Ever

22.

We are not
In the same boat
We have never
Been
In the same boat

Some of us are on
Cruise ships
With all possible
Comforts

Some
Are on
Makeshift boats
And might not
Even make it
To the shore

If you think
It is stupid
To talk about
Privilege
Then tell me
What boat
Are you on
And WHAT
Brought you
There

23.

When she
Who is White
Says
That they are
An honest family
*Una familia honrada*
When she says
That her husband
Who is Black
Is
An honest man
*Un hombre honrado*
And therefore
Therefore
They do not
Suffer
Racism
I do not ask
If she
Finds it okay
That others
Do
Suffer
Racism
If they
The others
Perhaps
Deserve

The racism
I do not ask
I let it go
But it stays there
Even later
At a distance
When we exchange
Messages
When we talk
On the phone
The unquestioned
Keeps hanging
Between us
And makes
All our conversations
Sound
Hollow

24.

I wish
I were
Prepared
Better equipped
More skilled
At
Interrupting
Racism

I wish
I could
Be
Proud
Of myself
For
Interrupting
Racism

I wish
I would not
Each time
Dwell
In guilt
And self-reproach
For not
Interrupting
Racism
Or not

Doing it
The right
Way

I wish
I could
Rewind
And make up
For each time
I did not
Interrupt
Racism

I wish
I wish
I wish
I were
Bolder
Louder
More audacious
Outspoken
Not ferocious
But unbroken
Articulate
Even humorous
With a sharp edge
And an attitude
To put people
In their place
Make them

Conscious
About race
Make them
Pause
And think
Defer the offense
Count to three
And swallow it
Again

25.

I remember
Your living room
You were so proud
Of your trips abroad
You had planned
Each one of them
In detail
Equipping yourself
With all sorts of
Paraphernalia
Only white folks
Seem to need
And you
Were
So proud
Of all
You brought back
So proud
That that dinner
Was meant
To show off
With your friends
Back in the city
And we
Were meant to say
Wow

I remember

Your living room
With horror
All those heads
Your camera had captured
As trophies of a hunt
All those heads exposed
In minimalistic frames
All over the place
And we
Meant to be sitting
At the dinner table
Attentive
To the accounts
Of your endeavours
Our mouths full
Our eyes wide open
Meaning
Wow

I remember
Your living room
And it still
Makes me sick
All those heads
From far-away places
All those souls
Stolen to their bodies
All those eyes
Watching us
White cannibals

Feasting
On tales
Of entitlement

I remember
Your living room
Myself blushing
With shame
Under the gaze
Of an old man
From Cappadocia
So much sadness
In his eyes
Behind the bars
of this human zoo of yours

I remember
Your living room
When it was dark
And the guests
Started to leave
I had a glimpse
Of the captives
Exchanging looks
And I thought to myself
You might possibly have
A rough night

26.

White-teen-me
Walked with you
Dear Qureisha
Recently arrived
From Somalia
A few years younger
Than myself
Chronologically
And yet
So much older
With the burden
Of history
On your shoulders

What did I know
What the hell did I know
And yet it was I
Who felt
I had something
To teach you
White-teen-me
With all the entitlement
Of racial supremacy

Oh I do not
Remember
What we
Talked about

Nor how
In what language
We understood
Each other
Nor if
We
Understood
Each other
At all

But I regret
Not listening
More closely
To your accounts
Your memories
Your experiences
Because I know
I did not listen enough
I know
I most likely dismissed
Your knowledge
And I was not even prepared
To acknowledge
Your wisdom

It was spring
And we
Were holding hands
During our walks
Through town

I wonder now
Why was that
Was I meant
To protect you
Or were we meant
To be like sisters
Because you would live
At my grandfather's place
For the next couple of years
Or was it simply
Because you were younger
And new to the place

You show her around
Said my mother
You teach her Italian
Said your mother
Be careful you two
Said my grandpa
So we set off
And I
Was officially
In charge

But what did I know
What the hell did I know

I wonder now
What you remember
Of those walks of ours

Were you scared
You did not seem to be
Your smile was genuine
And wide
And so beautiful
Not like mine
Hemmed in
By built-in hypocrisy
And self-consciousness
Were you amused
Or rather annoyed
At me
A white girl
With zero knowledge
Of the world
Chaperoning you
You
Who had wandered
On your own
Around Mogadishu
As rough as it was
Had now to be
Escorted
In the streets of Naples

Yet it was I
Who had
A big lesson
To learn
It was I

Who had
No idea
Of what my hometown
Looked like
And how rough
It could be
For someone
Your colour
It was I
Who burst into tears
My whole body shaking
After we ran away
That time
We were spat upon
And called names
And thrown things after
It was I
Who should have
Defended you
And protected you
And comforted you
And could not
Could not

What did I know
What the hell did I know
Did I really believe
Everybody would
Welcome you
Like my father had done

Preparing the papers
For you to come
Did I really believe
The whole town would
Smile benevolently
Like both our mothers
Waving at us from the balcony
Be careful you two
Had said my grandpa
And he knew better
He knew damn better

JCDecaux
UNITED COLORS
OF BENETTON.
vespa

27.

If I could rewind
And repair
I would go back
Twenty-five years
And an ocean
To make amends

A back yard
In a neighbourhood
On the outskirts of D.C.
A young woman
Sitting on the patio
A young man
Appearing in the garden

The woman
Barely concealing her alarm
Puts her book away
And starts to get inside

The man
Is quick
To apologise
And justify
His presence

So far so good

But the woman
Is white
Her alarm
Insanely predictable
And the man
Is black
His apology
A survival routine

Yet
Dear gentleman
In the back yard
I was the one
Who did not belong
Foreign to the place
In what was
Or should have been
Your
Territory

And your voice
Was so sincere
Your smile so true
And my shame
So deep
That even if
Our exchange
Was brief
You've lingered
In my memory

Ever since

And if I could rewind
And repair
I would go back
Twenty-five years
And an ocean
To make amends
And offer you
My apologies

28.

I've been writing
Silence poems
For a while
I've been writing
So many
One for each
Murder

Silence poems
Do not meet the page
Not even a blank space
They cannot
They would get it all
On fire

They get stocked
Instead
In the library
Of my heart
And I carry them
In my bosom
And rock them gently
And chant them softly
And polish them with care
And kiss them goodnight

And this is
At times

The only way
I can conceive
Of mourning
And honouring
The innocent lives
Lost to your brutality

Because there is
No poem
That could possibly
Meet the page
When a child
His hands up
Is shot in the chest




#AdamToledo

29.

Before
I did not even
Know
What
A Taser
Was

I am now
Learning
The vocabulary
Of brutality

Day by day
Murder after murder
My lexical knowledge
Expands

Death by death
Slaughter after slaughter
I get closer
To a level
Of proficiency
No language academy
Could have offered

I am packing
All those words
I am storing them

In a safe place
And when the time
Will come
I will take them out
And handle them
With the craft
Of the most skilled
Artisan

And that day
That day
Beware

I might decide
To set the timer
Or throw them
On the spot

And you'll have it
All
The Word
And the Bomb


#DaunteWright

30.

A child
In the body
Of an adult
A scared child
Who's lost sight
Of his dad
And is anxious
To get back to him
A child
Who panics
When the guard
Blocks his way

That is how
It all began

Except that
They did not see
The child
In you
They only
Saw
Your race
Which to them
Means
You are
A criminal
By default

And one
Unworthy
Of any regard
One
Against whom
Violence
Can be unleashed
All brutality
Is legitimate
No 'handle with care'
Required
Because you are
An outcast
A non-person
To them

So suddenly
You had four of them
on you
and then four more
As if you
A child
In the body
Of an adult
Were
A major threat
To gadjos' security

And now they say
Yours was

Death
By natural causes
No wonder
In a system
Where
Racism
Seems to be
As natural
As death


#EleazarGarcía

31.

Dear teacher
Not so dear
In fact
Don't you ever
Have regrets
For building
Walls
Around this child
Are you really
Persuaded
That you
Are being faithful
To your profession
By placing
Countless obstacles
In her path
And do you
Genuinely
Believe
That your whiteness
Has nothing
Really nothing
To do
With it

Oh no
Of course
You are not

Racist
Who
Would dare
To say
Such a thing
You
With your *schwarzen Patenkind*
As a token shield
And your *Indianer Heften*
As a badge of honour
For your openness
Are you really
So blind
To your own
Bigotry

Over the years
You've been stamping
This child
With your judgements
Unintelligent
Hyperactive
Conflictive
Paranoid
Narcissistic
And now
That her mother
Got her
Through multiple testing
And brought you

Scientifical proof
Of her skills
And potentials
Now you say
She is smart
So smart
So terribly smart
That she cannot
Possibly
Adapt
To your
Pedagogical
System

What next
What else
Will you come up with
To kick her out

Could anybody
Please remind
Educators
That the purpose
Of any school
Is to facilitate
Pupils' learning
And not
To make their life
Miserable
And that school

Is meant
To adapt
To pupils' needs
And not
The reverse

Dear teacher
Not so dear
In fact
How much more
Damage
Do you mean
To cause
You
Who are so keen
On writing protocols
And pathologizing
And making projections
About failures
And rejections
Don't you see
That you are acting
Pathologically
White
And yours is
The failure
For rejecting her
Instead of making her
Thrive

Stamped
From the beginning
Will she ever
Break free
Of the White grip
On her psyche
In this toxic battlefield
Such as school
Should never
Be

32.

Language
Is constantly
Changing
New words
Being coined
Old words
Being forgotten
Unusual words
Made familiar
Alien words
Getting adopted
Odd words
Getting adapted

The pandemic
Brought with it
A lexical upheaval
So sudden
Like a coup
And letting
No chance
For debate
And yet
We consented
And complied

Then why
I ask myself

Why is it
So difficult
For many of us
White folks
To repudiate
The language
Of violence
And subjugation

Why
Do we
Cling
So badly
To all our
N-words
And I-words
And P-words
The ABC
Of prejudice
And othering
All those punches
In the face
All those injuries
Denying
So many people
Of their individuality
And worth

When
Will we

Stop
Constructing
And defining
And restraining
And oppressing

When
Will we
Finally
Engage
In the downfall
Of racist
vocabulary

33.

You call it
Censorship
You dismiss it
As political correctness

I call it
Common sense
I call it
Respect
I call it
Antiracism

Oh
You call it
Cancel culture
But wait
Who cancelled
Whose culture
Were you not
The first and foremost
Canceler of cultures

I call it Counterculture
I call it Social Justice
I call it Antiracism

34.

At times
We fool
Ourselves
Into believing
There are
Some
Safe spaces
To talk
About race

But no space
Is entirely
Safe
As long as
White folks
Are around

Because
There is always
This one person
Blaming
Us
For being
Too radical
Too sensitive
Too demanding
Too everything

This woman today
Has managed to freeze
The virtual room
With her remarks

The micros were
Silenced
Yet in gallery view
One could see
The participants
Swallowing hard
And breathing deep
When she
Hurled the N-word
Loud and clear
Through our homes
And offices
Across Europe

My daughter
Was reading quietly
On the sofa
Behind me
And I wasn't
Quick enough
To put on
My earbuds
The damage
Had been done
The injury

Had entered
Our personal space

One wonders
How a scholar
With a sound
Background
On the subject
Can still
Accuse
Black people
Of censoring
And bashing
And excluding
Whites
And
Complain
Because
Because
She is not
Allowed
To say
The word
Anymore

But she did

35.

Every year
Around September
My mailbox is packed
With messages
From the school
And from other activities
The kids are involved in

Please confirm
Your consent
To pictures
Of your child
Being taken

or

If you object
To your child's image
Being shown
Please fill in and
Sign the form

And it's always
A bit of a dilemma
Because
You don't want
Your kids
To be used

As tokens
Of diversity
In Benetton style
Yet you also
Wish for
More visibility
For Children of Colour
In this all too White
World of ours

But then
When you
Sign and confirm
Your consent
Aren't you
Yourself
Opting for
Tokenism

So far
For the ambivalence
Of my racial
Predicament

36.

How many Tintin
Are still around
White guys
With extra-thin lips
And an ingrained
Sense of entitlement
Sticking their nose
Where it doesn't belong
Taking centre stage
As if it were a given
Making it clear
That they know better
They always
Know better
That's one of the
Assets
That comes
With Whiteness

How many Tintin
Are still around
And am I not
Am I not
Perhaps
One of them

37.

Whom
Am I talking to
If
Every time
I address
The subject
My interlocutors
Shy away
As if
I were bringing
News of death
And perhaps
Perhaps they are
Afraid
Just afraid
Of losing
Their Whiteness
With all its benefits
But what if
Most likely
They live
In denial
Of their (ours)
Chronic condition
And ward me off
In self-defence
Shall I still
Reach out

With a different
Hand
Or shall I
Keep still
And accept
My alienation
Choose your fights
I tell myself
It is only
That lately
All my fights
Bring loneliness
A deep
Aching
Loneliness
And I'm living
More and more
Inside myself
In this ocean
Of words and tears
Which is my mind

38.

After waving
Goodbye
To my children
At the school gate
I exchange a few words
With this new white mum
I am always so happy
When a Black child
Joins the school
I venture
And I've got
My very best smile
On me
Oh why
She exclaims alarmed
And she is already
Withdrawing
No
My daughter
Has never ever
Had
A problem
Well
I say
But still
It is nice
To have someone
Who looks

Like you
Yet I can see
In her eyes
That we sail
On different rivers
And I'd better
Smile politely
And leave it there

39.


Through months
Of home-schooling
And online classes
You witness first-hand
All the racist stuff
Your children get
From school
The compulsive
White saviourism
The ignorance of
All things African
The non-white bodies
As commodities
The supremacy
Of all things white
The appropriation
Of non-white cultures
The vestiges
Of plantation economy
And you are
Reminded
The urgency
Of doing
Counterculture
At home

40.

It must have been
Birthday number ten
I guess
The first one
With two numbers
Because my mum
Had bought
Two cakes
One white
One black
The white one
Was the face
Of the moon
The black one
The face of
Guess whom
Yes
Back in the early 80s
We were still
Cannibals
But choosy ones
We would only go
For black flesh
So that's how
I remember
That party
A bunch of
Wild White kids

Feasting over
A little N-cake
Tell me
Who the hell
Is the savage
Here




#BlackBodiesAreNotConsumables

41.

Not a carnival
Not a single
Carnival
Goes by
Without
An issue
After years
Of campaigning
By activists
Worldwide
Many still
Insist
In wearing
Racist costumes
And pretending
They are
Respectful
If not this
Then tell me
What is
Supremacy
Now they've been
Called out
For posting
A video tutorial
On dressing up as
And I'm called up
To offer

Elucidations
Which I do
Extensively
And without
Mincing my words
So I tell them
That First Nations
Are not one
But many cultures
I tell them
Of past
And present
Genocides
Look
What is
Happening
In Brazil
Right now
They are
Being
Killed
And you
Dress up
I tell them
Of symbolic
Violence
And cultural
Appropriation
I tell them
Intentions

Do not count
What does
Is the result
Which is
Racist
Plainly
Racist
I tell them
Creative freedom
Has nothing
Really nothing
To do
With it
And they
Should listen
To critical voices
And make amends
Instead of
Calling me
In the hope
I would justify
I tell them
They might rather
Propose
The costume
Of a local
Tribe
The Catalans
The Basques
And see

What happens
I tell them
There is no
Excuse
And they should
Withdraw
The video
And admit
They've acted
Against
The principles
They profess
But they
Have found
Quite a number
Of supporters
In the meantime
So they thank me
Politely
Keep the video
In place
And carry on
Acting
Racist
In denial
And I'm inclined
To see it
As a personal failure
In persuasion
Yet I must know

The stubbornness
Of supremacy
So deep-rooted
And hard
So hard
To eradicate

#MyCultureIsNotACostume

42.

The times
I am there
When I should not
The times
My presence
Is not acknowledged
The times
I witness
From a distance
My children's life
Without me
That is when I
Most deeply sense
The purport
Of my Whiteness
The extent
Of their vulnerability
The weight
Of all the prejudice
Associated
To being Black
And I'm filled
With anxiety
About their future
Will they find
A comfort zone
To be themselves
And safe

OPEN YOUR MIND
ASK THE NEXT PERSON
AND SHARE YOUR INSP
TRAVEL OFTE
SOME OPPORTU
LIFE IS ABOU
THE THINGS
SO GO OU
LIFE IS
SHORT
VERY LAST BITE.

43.

If all lives matter
As you say
Then
Start from the children
Start teaching them
Showing them
That
They all
Matter
Because you see
In your world
We do not see
That our children
Matter that much
We do not see
Our children
In your books
If not as
Caricatures
Tokens
Gap-fillings
We do not see
Our children
In your schools
If not as
That much blessed
Exception
Appearing

On all photographs
We do not see
Our children
In your films
If not as
The problem
We do not see
Our children
In your toys
If not as
Savages
We do not see them
We do not see
And until
The day we will
Don't you dare
Tell us
That
All lives
Matter

44.

Our children
Are in your ghettos
Our children
Are in your prisons
Our children
Are in your graveyards
Let them be safe first
Let them be children
Let them be
And then we can talk

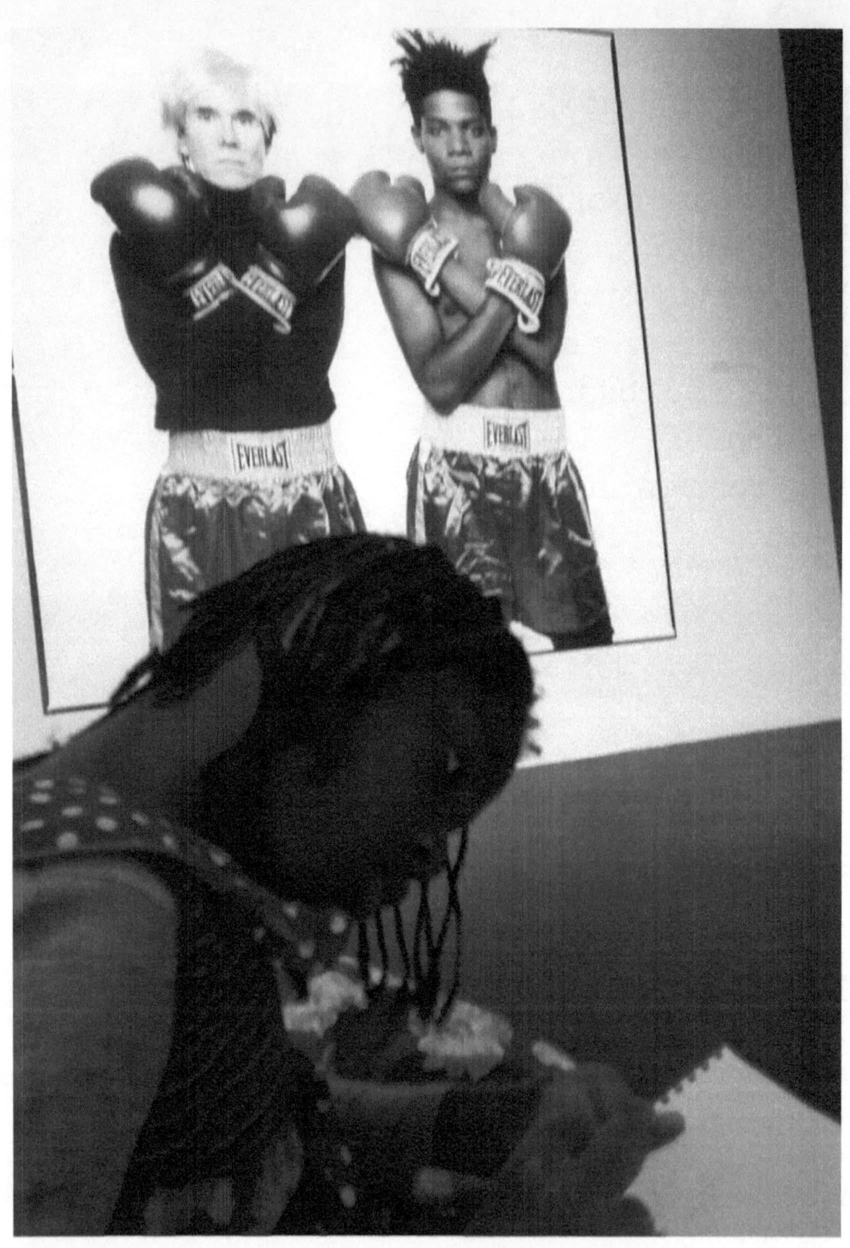

45.

You do not have
To worry
About race
Every day
Every moment
Of your life
That is
Your privilege
You do not have
To think
Of yourself
As a racialised being
In fact you belong
To the invisible race
That is
Your privilege
You do not have
To see yourself
As the projection
Others have made
Of you
That is
Your privilege
You do not have
To fear
For your life
Because of the colour
Of your skin

That is
Your privilege
You do not have
To enter a shop
Feeling you are
Suspicious
That is
Your privilege
You do not have
To carry
Your identity papers
On you
All the time
That is
Your privilege
You do not have
To lose sleep
About not getting
Proper medical treatment
That is
Your privilege
You do not have
To look
For a special hairdresser
To care for your hair
That is
Your privilege
You do not have
To justify
Your presence

To be
Hyper conscious
To watch
Your behaviour
All the time
That is
Your privilege
You do not have
To prove
You are worthy
To state
You belong
To show
You are inoffensive
That is
Your privilege
You do not have
To weigh
Your words
Every single one
For fear of hurting
Sensibilities
And being targeted
As the one
Who's playing
The race card
That is
Your privilege
You do not have
To be the first

The best
The outstanding
And still feel
You are
The last
The worst
The insignificant
You do not have
You do not have
You do not have
To wear your skin
Like a burden
That is
Your privilege
And a million others

46.

White like me
You pretend
You do not see
Colour
Nor
Of course
Racism
Yet your every
Interaction
Is tainted by
Plantation memories

White like me
You pretend
You cannot be
Anything other
Than liberal
And progressive
Yet you are stuck
In your privilege
And refuse to give up
The tiniest bit

White like me
You pretend
You don't agree
With any form
Of discrimination

Yet you seem
Incapable
Of conducting
A simple conversation
Without stigmatizing
One or the other group

White like me
Let me tell you
You still have
A long way to go
In unlearning race
A long way to go
In falling out
Of whiteness
A long way to go
In becoming
An ally
For real

47.

You own
Every single space
You occupy
Oblivious
Of this privilege
Denied
To many others

You own
The restaurant
The cinema
The art gallery
The beach
The train station
The police department
The street
No matter the code
No matter the country

You even own
Our ghetto
Our music
Our art
Our hair

You even own
All those spaces
When you travel

Abroad

Yet you
Are
The numerical
Minority
Here

Whites do not
Make up
Seventeen per cent
Of the total
World population

Then how comes
You seem to own
The whole world

Redress
My friend
Redress

48.

We are quick
To blame them
And to point out
We are not
Involved
(we don't believe it
ourselves
do we)
And what perverse
Pleasure
We take
In talking about it
As if we were really
Not
Involved
We say
Black on Black violence
As if our violence
Had no colour
We say
Black on Asian hate crimes
As if hate
Had not come
From us first
We talk about
Ethnic conflicts
As if it were not us
In the first place

Who made them tribal
(how fine we have
regional frictions instead
and our wars are
civil)
We delight
In enumerating
Examples of colourism
(wait
is this a joke
do we really believe
this has nothing to do
with us)
And other nonsensical
Terms and concepts
We created
To divest ourselves
Of responsibility
And that are
Nothing more
Than expressions
Of our own
Racism
And euphemisms
For its side effects
And as long as we don't see
The supremacy implied
We will be stuck
In guilt

AUX DELICATES ECAILLES ARGENT
ETAIT NETTEMENT LES ANTENNES
MATERNELLES FORMAIENT UN
LA GOSSELINE POUR ALLER
MOI DEMENAGE DE L'AVENUE
NOUS AVIONS MA MERE ET
A LA MORT DE MON PERE
LITTORAL CARAIBEEN D'HAITI
A JACMEL LOCALITE DU
DE MON ENFANCE JE VIVAIS
CETTE ANNEE LA, A LA FIN

49.

And now
We talk about
Imperialism
And point the finger
At the Chinese
It's remarkable
How Whiteness
Reinvents itself
All the time
Invested with
Innocence
Legitimacy
Superiority
How can I
Find myself
In this body
And become
Someone else
Altogether

50.

Insidious by design
My race pops up
At every corner
It might be invisible
But not innocent
And hardly ever
Innocuous
A thought pushed back
The memory of an old fantasy
A revealing glance
An unreflective comment
The way I own the space
Or don't
A picture taken
A stupid assumption
A vote cast too quickly
A sense of entitlement
A self-defensive response
An arrogant blindness
Some sort of condescension
My sheer parenthood
The way I match the background
Or don't
My silence
Insidious by design
And more
Much more
Than the shades

Of my complexion
My race exudes
Through all my pores
As centuries of supremacy
Have gone deep
In shaping my identity
But I will not comply
And you shouldn't
Either

And yes, we are falling out, but we have not made it
through.
Antiracism is a task for a lifetime.

Dear Reader,
If this book has stirred something and changed your
perspective, even if only a tiny bit, please send me a word.
I would love to hear from you.
You can reach me at: brancatosabrina@gmail.com

# A few words about myself

Born on Mediterranean shores, I was that kind of solitary child who would spend hours reading or daydreaming. Later, I developed into a solitary adult who would spend hours reading and daydreaming.

Following a thread marked by the written worlds I navigated, I chose to dig deep into literary studies and developed a passion for postcolonial literatures for bringing forward a sense of justice that was too often absent from what I saw around me. When I went into teaching, it was to share the inspiration and knowledge received by the authors who most influenced me. When I went into writing, it was to share my vision of the world, how it is in my eyes and how I would like it to be.

To acknowledge the multiple cultural backgrounds making up my identity and the many languages I write in or draw from, I like to call myself MELTING POèT. Poetry is for me a form of micro-activism. My poems will not be able to change racist policies for antiracist ones, but they might produce some important change nonetheless. By reaching people's emotions and understanding, I hope to contribute to bringing antiracist ideas and practices into the mainstream and pushing all forms of bigotry to the margins.

# Other books by the same author

*Where Whiteness Fears to Tread: Lyrics on Race*
(KDP, 2020)

*Chocolindo en el país de las escobas y otros cuentos*
(KDP, 2019)

*Farafinna: Images, paysages et visages*
(KDP, 2018)

*Sono nero e sono fiero e altre filastrocche e poesie giocose*
(KDP, 2017)

*Afroeurope@n Configurations: Readings and Projects* (ed.)
Cambridge Scholar Publishing (2011)

*Afro-Europe: Texts and Contexts*
Trafo Verlag (2009)

*Ancor ci si imbaRAZZA: Storie di ordinaria xenofollia*
Besa Editrice (2008)

*Mother and Motherland in Jamaica Kincaid*
Peter Lang (2005)

www.sabrinabrancato.com